Alfred's
Easy guitar songs

MW00861215

CHRISTMAS

50 HOLIDAY FAVORITES

Produced by
Alfred Music
P.O. Box 10003
Van Nuys, CA 91410-0003
alfred.com

Printed in USA.

ISBN-10: 1-4706-3614-X
ISBN-13: 978-1-4706-3614-2

Cover Photos
Gibson Hummingbird courtesy of Gibson Brands • Duesenberg Dragster DC courtesy of Duesenberg Guitars, USA

Alfred Cares. Contents printed on environmentally responsible paper.

contents

TITLE	PAGE

TITLE	PAGE

STRUM PATTERNS

Below are a number of suggested patterns that may be used while strumming the chords for the songs in this book. Think of these as starting points from which you may embellish, mix up, or create your own patterns.

Note the markings above the staff that indicate the direction of the strums.

⊓ indicates a downstroke

V indicates an upstroke

FINGERPICKING PATTERNS

Here are some fingerpicking patterns that may be used to arpeggiate chords where indicated in this book.
As with the strum patterns, these are starting points from which you may embellish, mix up, or create your own patterns.

Note the fingerings:
p = thumb
i = index finger
m = middle finger
a = ring finger

⊓ indicates a downstroke   ⋁ indicates an upstroke

Fingerpicking Pattern #1:

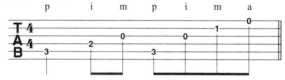

Fingerpicking Pattern #2:

Fingerpicking Pattern #3:

Fingerpicking Pattern #4:

Fingerpicking Pattern #5:

Fingerpicking Pattern #6:

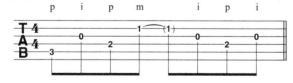

Fingerpicking Pattern #7:

Fingerpicking Pattern #8:

Fingerpicking Pattern #9:

Fingerpicking Pattern #10:

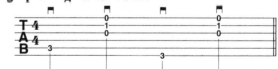

Fingerpicking Pattern #11:

Fingerpicking Pattern #12:

Fingerpicking Pattern #13:

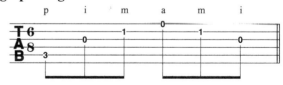

Fingerpicking Pattern #14:

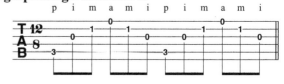

ANGELS WE HAVE HEARD ON HIGH

Use Suggested Strum Pattern #3

Traditional Carol

Brightly

AWAY IN A MANGER

Use Suggested Strum Pattern #8
or Fingerpicking Pattern #8

Music by
JAMES R. MURRAY

Bright waltz

cattle are low-ing, the poor ba-by wakes. But____
way in a man-ger no crib for His bed. The____

lit-tle Lord Je-sus, no cry-ing He makes. I
lit-tle Lord Je-sus lay down His sweet head. The

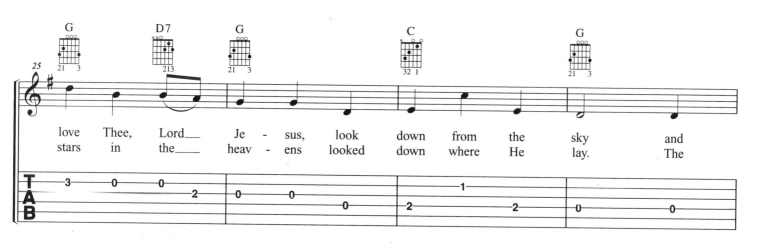

love Thee, Lord____ Je-sus, look down from the sky and
stars in the____ heav-ens looked down down from where He sky lay. The

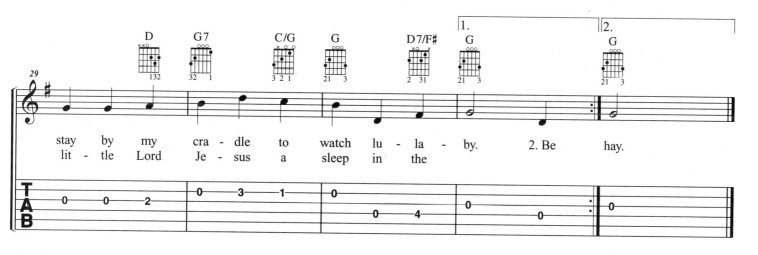

stay by my cra-dle to watch lu-la-by. 2. Be hay.
lit-tle Lord Je-sus a sleep in the

Away in a Manger - 2 - 2

BELIEVE
(from *The Polar Express*)

**Use Suggested Strum Pattern #3
or Fingerpicking Pattern #1**

Words and Music by
ALAN SILVESTRI and GLEN BALLARD

Moderately slow
Verse:

Believe - 3 - 1

BRING A TORCH, JEANNETTE, ISABELLA

Use Suggested Strum Pattern #9
or Fingerpicking Pattern #8

Traditional French Carol

BLUE CHRISTMAS

Use Suggested Strum Pattern #6

Moderate swing feel

Words and Music by
BILL HAYES and JAY JOHNSON

Chorus:
I'll have a blue Christ-mas with-out you. ___ I'll be so blue think-ing a-bout you. ___ Dec-o-

Bridge:
ra - tions of red on a green Christ-mas tree won't mean a thing if you're not here with me. ___ I'll have a

Blue Christmas - 2 - 1

CELEBRATE ME HOME

Lyrics by
KENNY LOGGINS

Music by
KENNY LOGGINS
and BOB JAMES

Use Suggested Strum Pattern #8
Moderately

Verse 1:

Home___ for the hol - i - days, I be - lieve I've missed each and ev - 'ry face. Come on and play one eas - y.___ Let's turn on ev - 'ry love light in the place.___ It's time I found my - self to - tal - ly sur - round - ed in your cir - cles.___ Oh,___ my friends,___

Celebrate Me Home - 5 - 1

A CHILD THIS DAY IS BORN

**Use Suggested Strum Pattern #8
or Fingerpicking Pattern #8**

Words and Music by
WILLIAM SANDYS

Verse 3:
And as the angel told them,
So to them did appear.
They found the young Child, Jesus Christ,
With Mary, his Mother dear.
(To Chorus:)

CHRISTMAS VACATION
(from *National Lampoon's Christmas Vacation*)

Use Suggested Strum Pattern #6

Moderately

Verses 1 & 2:

Words and Music by
BARRY MANN and CYNTHIA WEIL

Christmas Vacation - 3 - 1

THE COVENTRY CAROL

Use Suggested Strum Pattern #9
or Fingerpicking Pattern #8

Traditional English Carol

Moderate waltz

Verse 3:
Herod the king in his raging,
Charged he hath this day.
His men of might, in his own sight,
All children young to slay.

Verse 4:
Then woe is me, poor Child, for thee,
And ever mourn and say.
For Thy parting nor say nor sing,
Bye, bye, lulloo, lullay.

DECK THE HALL

Traditional Welsh Carol

Strum Pattern should basically follow rhythm of melody

DO YOU HEAR WHAT I HEAR?

Words and Music by
NOEL REGNEY and GLORIA SHAYNE

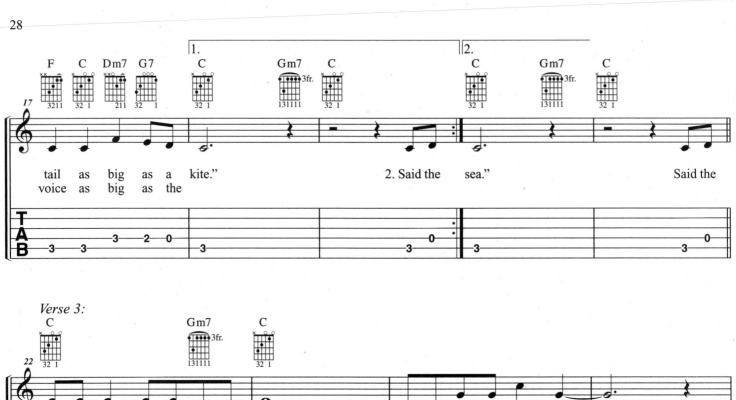

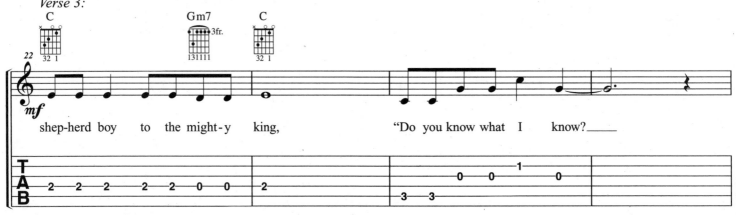

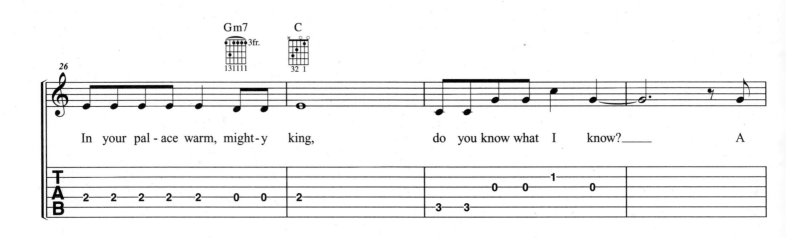

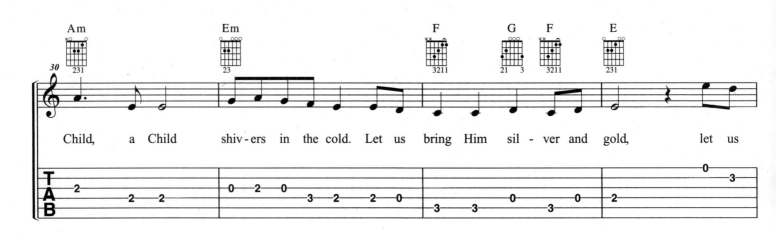

THE FIRST NOEL

Use Suggested Strum Pattern #8

Traditional Carol

GO TELL IT ON THE MOUNTAIN

Use Suggested Strum Pattern #3

Fast

Traditional Spiritual

Verse 3:
While shepherds kept their watching
O'er wand'ring flock by night,
Behold, from out the Heavens
There shown a holy light.
(To Chorus:)

Verse 4:
And lo, when they had seen it,
They all bowed down and prayed.
Then they travelled on together,
To where the Babe was laid.
(To Chorus:)

THE FRIENDLY BEASTS

**Use Suggested Strum Pattern #9
or Fingerpicking Pattern #8**

Traditional English Carol

Moderate waltz

Verses 1–3:

1. Je - sus, our broth - er____ kind____ and__ good,____ was hum - bly
2. "I," said the don - key,____ shag - gy and__ brown,____ "I car - ried His
3. *See additional lyrics*

born in a sta - ble of wood. And the friend - ly beasts a -
moth - er up - hill and down. I car - ried her safe - ly to

round him stood, Je - sus, our__ broth - er kind____ and
Beth - le - hem town. I," said the don - key, shag - gy and

1.2.
C   G7
good.
brown.

3.
C   F   G   A   G/B   A/C#
red.

The Friendly Beasts - 2 - 1

Verse 3:
"I," said the cow, all white and red,
"I gave Him my manger for a bed.
I gave Him my hay to pillow His head.
I," said the cow, all white and red.
(To Verse 4:)

Verse 6:
"I," said the camel, yellow and black,
"Over the desert upon my back,
I brought Him a gift in the wise man's pack.
I," said the camel, yellow and black.

Verse 7:
And thus, every beast, remembering it well,
In the stable dark was so proud to tell,
Of the gifts that they gave Emmanuel.
The gifts that they gave Emmanuel.

GESU BAMBINO
(The Infant Jesus)

English Lyrics by
FREDERICK H. MARTENS

Music and Italian Lyrics by
PIETRO A. YON

Use Suggested Strum Pattern #13

Gesu Bambino (The Infant Jesus) - 2 - 1

THE GIFT

Use Suggested Strum Pattern #6
or Fingerpicking Pattern #4

Slowly

Words and Music by
JIM BRICKMAN and TOM DOUGLAS

The Gift - 4 - 1

38

The Gift - 4 - 3

GOD REST YE MERRY, GENTLEMEN

Use Suggested Strum Pattern #14

Traditional Carol

God Rest Ye Merry, Gentlemen - 2 - 1

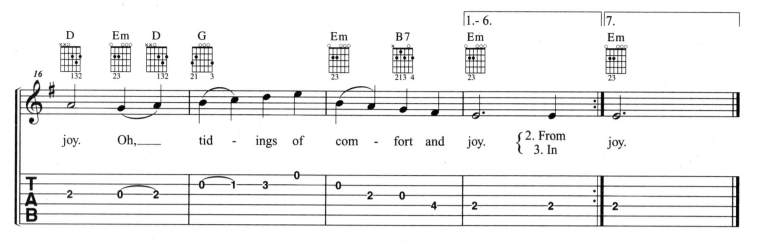

Verse 3:
In Bethlehem, in Jewry,
This Blessed Babe was born.
And laid within a manger
Upon this holy morn,
The which his Mother Mary
Did nothing take in scorn.
Oh, tidings…

Verse 4:
"Fear not then," said the angel,
"Let nothing you affright.
This day is born a Savior,
Of a pure Virgin bright,
To free all those who trust in Him
From Satan's power and might."
Oh, tidings…

Verse 5:
The shepherds at those tidings
Rejoiced much in mind,
And left their flocks a-feeding
In tempest, storm, and wind,
And went to Bethlehem straightway,
The Son of God to find.
Oh, tidings…

Verse 6:
And when they came to Bethlehem
Where our dear Savior lay,
They found Him in a manger
Where oxen feed on hay.
His Mother Mary kneeling down,
Unto the Lord did pray.
Oh, tidings…

Verse 7:
Now to the Lord sing praises,
All you within this place.
And with true love and brotherhood
Each other now embrace.
This holy tide of Christmas
All other doth deface.
Oh, tidings…

GOOD KING WENCESLAS

Words by
JOHN M. NEALE

Traditional Carol

Use Suggested Strum Pattern #14

Moderately

Verse 3:
"Bring me flesh and bring me wine, bring me pine logs hither.
Thou and I will see him dine, when we bear him thither."
Page and monarch forth they went, forth they went together,
Through the rude wind's wild lament and the bitter weather.

Verse 4:
"Sire, the night is darker now, and the wind blows stronger.
Fails my heart, I know not how, I can go no longer."
"Mark my footsteps, my good page, tread thou in them boldly.
Thou shalt find the winter's rage freeze thy blood less coldly."

Verse 5:
In his master's steps he trod, where the snow lay dinted.
Heat was in the very sod which the Saint had printed.
Therefore, Christian men, be sure, wealth or rank possessing;
Ye who will now bless the poor shall yourselves find blessing.

HARK! THE HERALD ANGELS SING

Traditional Carol

**Use Suggested Strum Pattern #14
or Fingerpicking Pattern #5**

Moderately

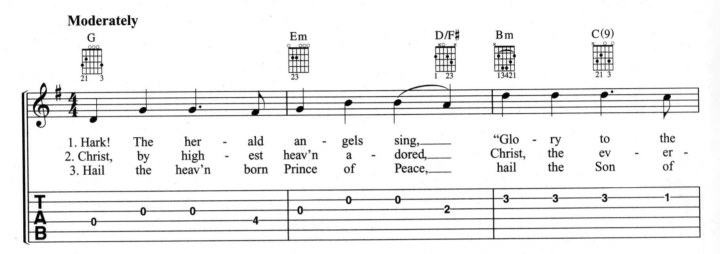

1. Hark! The her - ald an - gels sing,____ "Glo - ry to the
2. Christ, by high - est heav'n a - dored,____ Christ, the ev - er -
3. Hail by the heav'n born Prince of Peace,____ hail the Son of

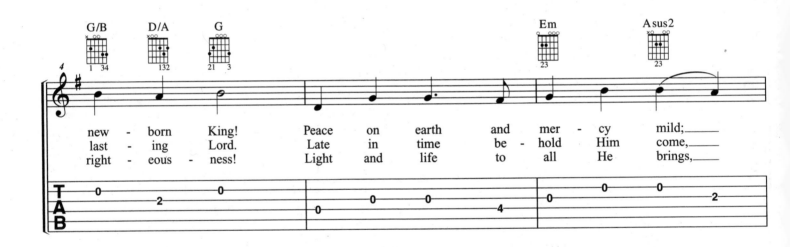

new - born King! Peace on earth and mer - cy mild;____
last - ing Lord. Late in time be - hold Him come,____
right - eous - ness! Light and life to all He brings,____

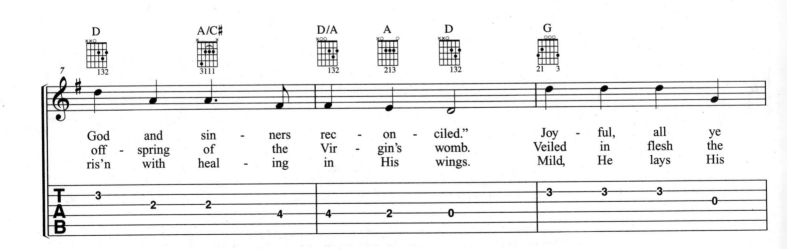

God and sin - ners rec - on - ciled." Joy - ful, all ye
off - spring of the Vir - gin's womb. Veiled in flesh the
ris'n with heal - ing in His wings. Mild, He lays His

Hark! The Herald Angels Sing - 2 - 1

Hark! The Herald Angels Sing - 2 - 2

HAVE YOURSELF A MERRY LITTLE CHRISTMAS

Words and Music by
HUGH MARTIN and RALPH BLANE

Use Suggested Strum Pattern #3
or Finderpicking Pattern #1

Have Yourself a Merry Little Christmas - 2 - 1

A HOLLY JOLLY CHRISTMAS

Words and Music by
JOHNNY MARKS

Use Suggested Strum Pattern #12

Bright two-beat

A Holly Jolly Christmas - 2 - 1

A Holly Jolly Christmas - 2 - 2

(There's No Place Like)
HOME FOR THE HOLIDAYS

Words by
AL STILLMAN

Music by
ROBERT ALLEN

(There's No Place Like) Home for the Holidays - 2 - 1

(There's No Place Like) Home for the Holidays - 2 - 2

I HEARD THE BELLS ON CHRISTMAS DAY

Words by
HENRY WADSWORTH LONGFELLOW

Music by
JOHN BAPTISTE CALKIN

Use Suggested Strum Pattern #2
Moderately

I'LL BE HOME FOR CHRISTMAS

Words by
KIM GANNON

Music by
WALTER KENT

Use Suggested Strum Pattern #3

Moderately

IT CAME UPON THE MIDNIGHT CLEAR

Use Suggested Strum Pattern #9
or Fingerpicking Pattern #9

Traditional Carol

Medium waltz

It Came Upon the Midnight Clear - 2 - 1

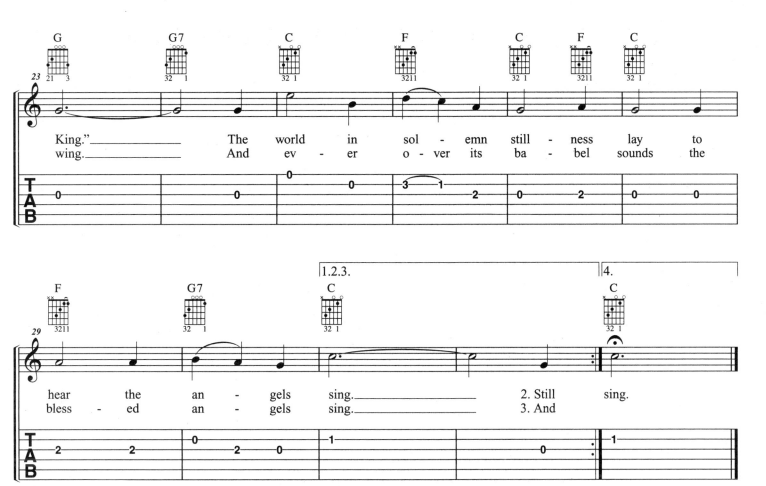

Verse 3:
And ye beneath life's crushing load,
Whose forms are bending low,
Who toil along the climbing way,
With painful steps and slow,
Look now! For glad and golden hours
Come swiftly on the wing.
O rest beside the weary road
And hear the angels sing.

Verse 4:
For lo, the days are hast'ning on,
By prophet bards foretold.
When, with the evercircling years,
Comes 'round the age of gold,
When peace shall over all the earth
Its ancient splendor fling,
And the whole world give back the song
Which now the angels sing.

IT'S THE MOST WONDERFUL
TIME OF THE YEAR

**Use Suggested
Strum Pattern #8**

Words and Music by
EDDIE POLA and
GEORGE WYLE

Bright waltz

It's the Most Wonderful Time of the Year - 2 - 1

JINGLE BELLS

Suggested Strum Pattern #3

Brightly

Words and Music by
JAMES PIERPONT

Jingle Bells - 2 - 1

JOLLY OLD SAINT NICHOLAS

Use Suggested Strum Pattern #12

Traditional American Carol

JOY TO THE WORLD

Words by
ISAAC WATTS

Music by
G. F. HANDEL

Use Suggested Strum Pattern #12

Brightly

1. Joy to the world! The Lord is come. Let earth re-
2. Joy to the world! The Sav - ior reigns. Let men their
3. He rules the world with truth and grace, and makes the

ceive her King. Let ev - 'ry heart pre - pare Him
songs em - ploy. While field and floods, rocks, hills, and
na - tions prove the glo - ries of His right - eous -

room, and heav'n and na - ture sing, and heav'n and na - ture sing, and
plains re - peat the sound - ing joy, re - peat the sound - ing joy, re -
ness, and won - ders of His love, and won - ders of His love, and

heav'n and heav'n and na - ture sing. love.
peat, re - peat the sound - ing joy.
won - ders, won - ders of His

THE LITTLE DRUMMER BOY

Words and Music by
HARRY SIMEONE, HENRY ONORATI
and KATHERINE DAVIS

Use Intro as suggested strum pattern
Slow with a march feel

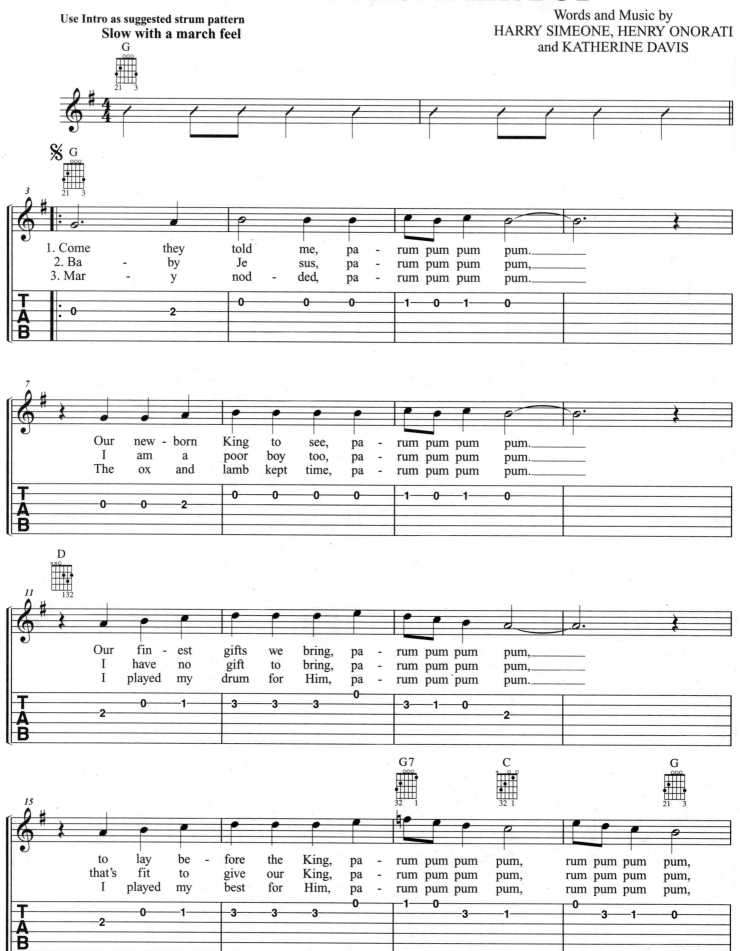

The Little Drummer Boy - 2 - 1

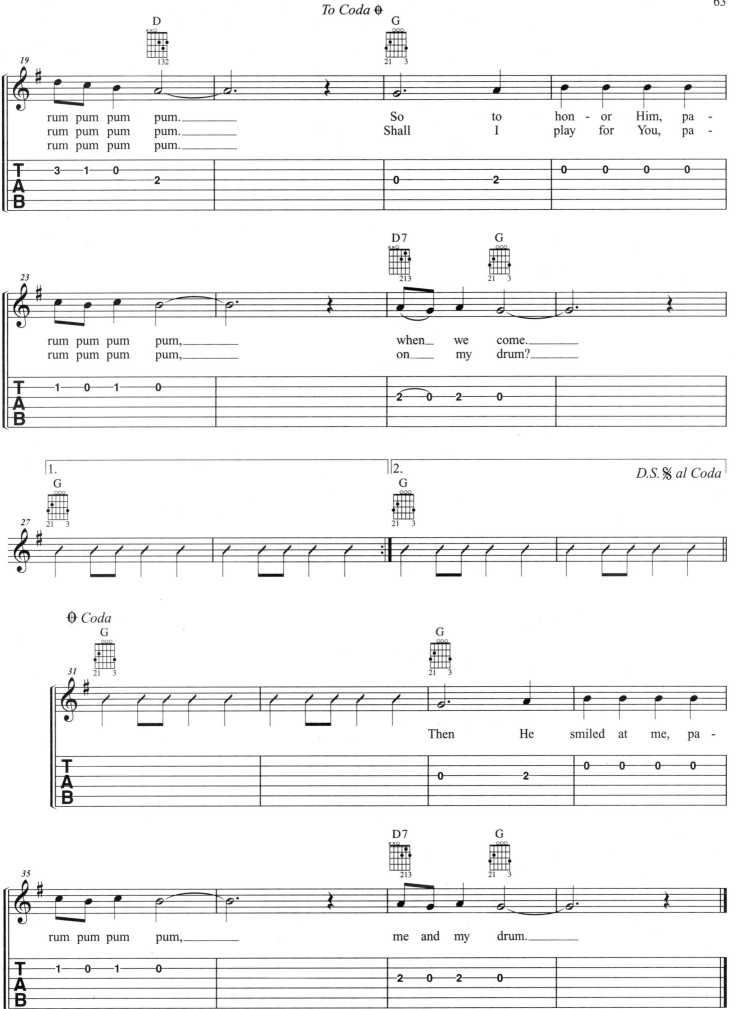

The Little Drummer Boy - 2 - 2

MELE KALIKIMAKA

Use Suggested Strum Pattern #14

Words and Music by
R. ALEX ANDERSON

Brightly

O CHRISTMAS TREE

(O Tannenbaum)

Traditional Carol

Use Suggested Strum Pattern #8

Moderate waltz

O COME, ALL YE FAITHFUL
(Adeste Fideles)

English Words by
FREDERICK OAKELEY
Latin Words Attributed to
JOHN FRANCIS WADE

Music by
JOHN READING

**Use Suggested Strum Pattern #14
or Fingerpicking Pattern #3**

O HOLY NIGHT

**Use Suggested Strum Pattern #15
or fingerpick as shown in bar 1**

Words and Music by
J. S. DWIGHT and ADOLPHE ADAM

O Holy Night - 2 - 1

O Holy Night - 2 - 2

O LITTLE TOWN OF BETHLEHEM

Words by
PHILLIPS BROOKS

Music by
LEWIS H. REDNER

**Use Suggested Strum Pattern #6
or Fingerpicking Pattern #2**

Moderately

SILENT NIGHT

**Use Suggested Strum Pattern #9
or Fingerpicking Pattern #9**

Moderate waltz

Words and Music by
JOSEPH MOHR and
FRANZ GRUBER

1. Si - lent night, ho - ly night, all is calm,
2. Si - lent night, ho - ly night, shep - herds quake
3. Si - lent night, ho - ly night, Son of God,

all is bright. 'Round yon Vir - gin Moth - er and Child.
at the sight. Glo - ries stream__ from heav - en a - far.
love's pure light. Ra - diant beams__ from Thy ho - ly face,

Ho - ly In - fant so ten - der and mild. Sleep in heav - en - ly
Heav - 'nly hosts__ sing Al - le - lu - ia. Christ the Sav - ior is
with the dawn of re - deem - ing grace. Je - sus Lord at Thy

peace,_____ sleep__ in heav - en - ly peace! birth!
born!_____ Christ__ the Sav - ior is born!
birth._____ Je - sus Lord at Thy

ROCKIN' AROUND THE CHRISTMAS TREE

Words and Music by
JOHNNY MARKS

Use Suggested Strum Pattern #3

Lively rock and roll

Rock-in' a-round the Christ-mas tree___ at the
Christ-mas par-ty hop.___ Mis-tle-toe hung where you can see___ ev-'ry
cou-ple tries to stop. Rock-in' a-round the Christ-mas tree___ let the
Christ-mas spir-it ring.___ Lat-er we'll have some pump-kin pie___ and we'll

Rockin' Around the Christmas Tree - 2 - 1

UDOLPH, THE RED-NOSED REINDEER

Words and Music by
JOHNNY MARKS

Use Suggested Strum Pattern #3

SANTA CLAUS IS COMIN' TO TOWN

Music by
J. FRED COOTS

Santa Claus Is Comin' to Town - 2 - 1

Santa Claus Is Comin' to Town - 2 - 2

SILVER AND GOLD

**Use Suggested Strum Pattern #9
or Fingerpicking Pattern #9**

Words and Music by
JOHNNY MARKS

TEXT ME MERRY CHRISTMAS

Use Suggested Strum Pattern #4

Words and Music by
DAVID JAVERBAUM and
ADAM SCHLESINGER

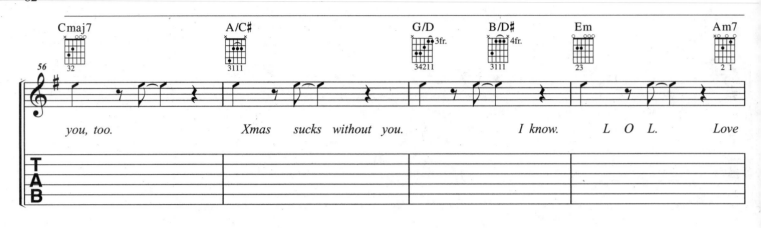

you, too. *Xmas sucks without you.* *I know.* *L O L.* Love

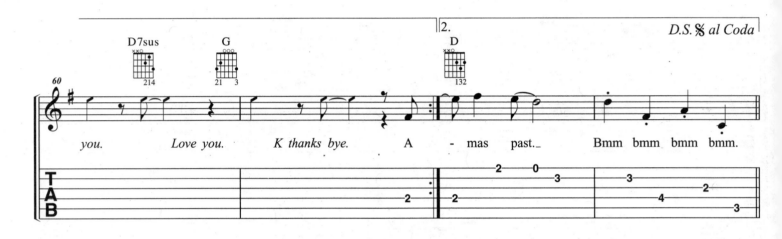

you. *Love you.* *K thanks bye.* A - mas past. Bmm bmm bmm bmm.

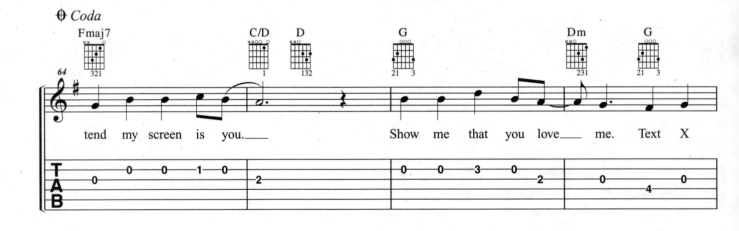

tend my screen is you. Show me that you love me. Text X

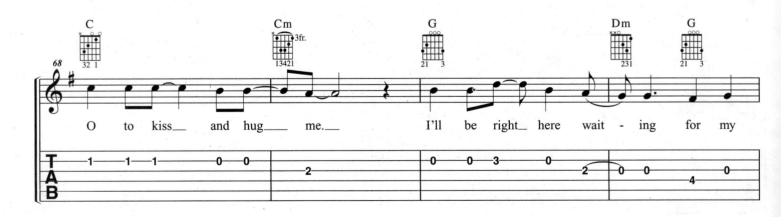

O to kiss and hug me. I'll be right here wait - ing for my

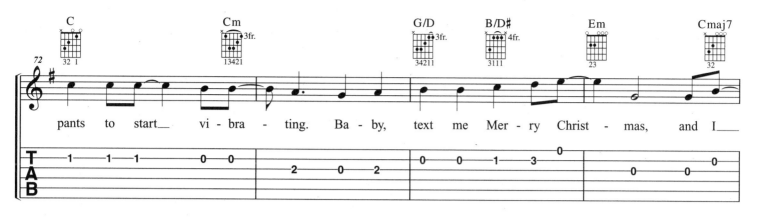

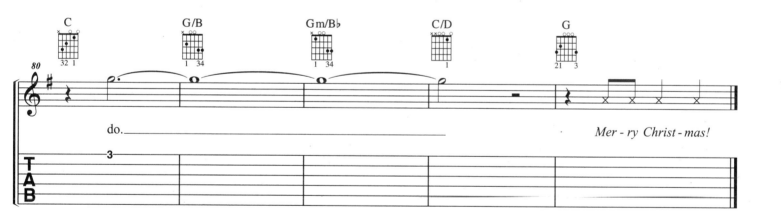

Bridge 2:
A Facebook message isn't quite as sweet.
I need more from @ you than just a tweet.
A snap on snapchat doesn't last, and voicemail,
That's from Christmas past.
Bmm bmm bmm bmm.

Chorus 2:
Text me Merry Christmas.
Send a selfie, too.
If you do, I'll go 'neath the mistletoe
And pretend my screen is you.
(To Coda)

SLEIGH RIDE

Words by
MITCHELL PARISH

Music by
LEROY ANDERSON

Sleigh Ride - 4 - 1

THE TWELVE DAYS OF CHRISTMAS

Use Suggested Strum Pattern #14

Traditional English Carol

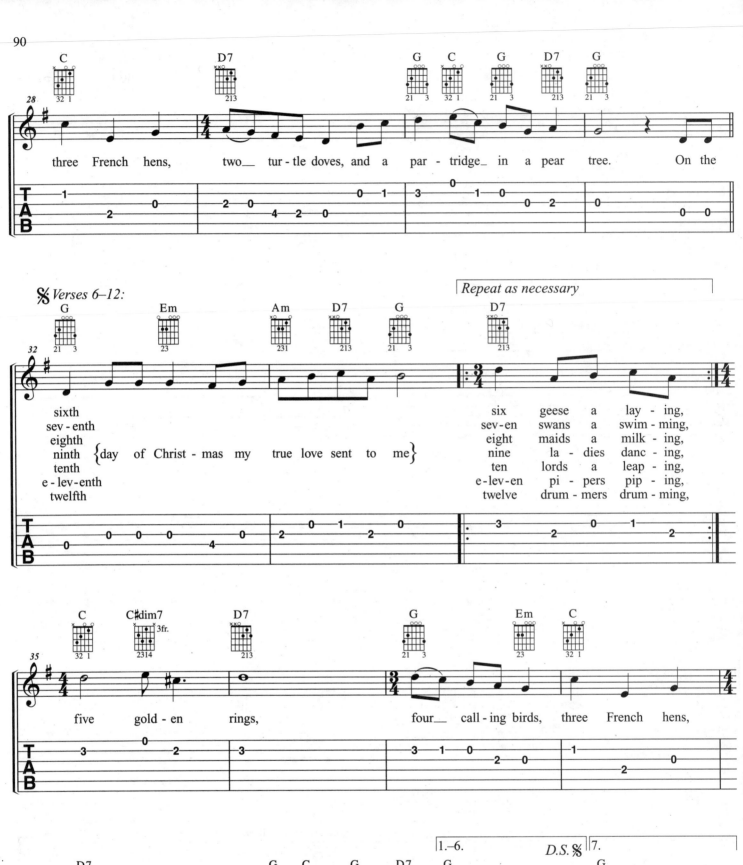

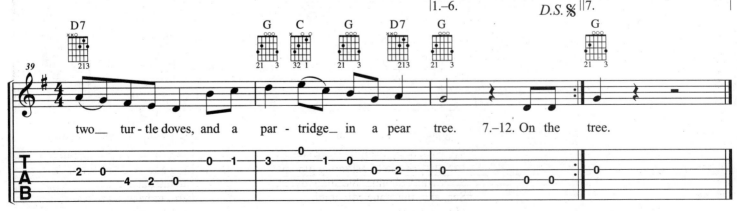

WE THREE KINGS OF ORIENT ARE

Words and Music by
JOHN H. HOPKINS

Use Suggested Strum Pattern #9

Moderate waltz

1. We three kings of O - ri - ent are, bear - ing gifts, we tra - verse a -
2. Born a king on Beth - le - hem's plain, gold I bring to crown Him a -
3.–5. *See additional lyrics*

far. Field and foun - tain, moor and moun - tain, fol - low - ing yon - der star.
gain. King for - ev - er, ceas - ing nev - er, o - ver us all to reign.

Chorus:

O,___ star of won - der, star of night, star with roy - al beau - ty bright,

west - ward lead - ing, still pro - ceed - ing, guide us to Thy per - fect light. light.

Verse 3:
Frankincense to offer have I,
Incense owns a deity nigh.
Prayer and praising, all men raising,
Worship Him, God most high.
(To Chorus:)

Verse 4:
Myrrh is mine: its bitter perfume
Breathes of life of gathering gloom;
Sorrowing, sighing, bleeding, dying,
Sealed in the stone cold tomb.
(To Chorus:)

Verse 5:
Glorious now behold Him arise;
King and God and sacrifice.
Alleluia, alleluia,
Earth to heaven replies.
(To Chorus:)

UKRAINIAN BELL CAROL

Composed by
MYKOLA LEONTOVYCH

Use Suggested Strum Pattern #8

Joyfully

Ukrainian Bell Carol - 2 - 1

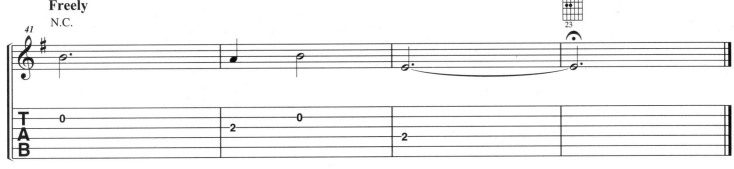

WE WISH YOU A MERRY CHRISTMAS

Use Suggested Strum Pattern #10
Medium waltz

Traditional English Folk Song

WHAT CHILD IS THIS?

(Greensleeves)

By
WILLIAM C. DIX

**Use Suggested Strum Pattern #9
or Fingerpicking Pattern #13**

Gently

Am C G Em Am F E E7

1. What child is this__ who laid to rest__ on Mar - y's lap__ is sleep - ing? Whom
lies He in__ such mean es - tate__ where ox and ass__ are feed - ing? Good
bring Him in - cense, gold, and myrrh, come peas - ant king to own Him. The

Am C G Em Am E7 Am

an - gels greet__ with an - thems sweet,__ while shep - herds watch__ are keep - ing?
Chris - tian, fear__ for sin - ners here,__ the si - lent Word__ is plead - ing.
King of Kings,__ sal - va - tion brings;__ let lov - ing hearts__ en - throne Him.

C Em G Em Am F E E7

This, this__ is Christ the King;__ Whom shep - herds guard__ and an - gels sing:
Nails, spears__ shall pierce Him through,__ the cross be borne__ for me, for you.
Raise, raise__ the song on high,__ the Vir - gin sings__ her lul - la - by.

C Em G Em Am E7 1.2. Am 3. Am

Haste, haste__ to bring Him laud,__ the Babe,__ the Son__ of Mar - y! 2. Why Mar - y!
Hail, hail__ the Word made flesh,__ the Babe,__ the Son__ of Mar - y! 3. So
Joy, joy__ for Christ is born,__ the Babe,__ the Son__ of

WELCOME CHRISTMAS
(from *How The Grinch Stole Christmas*)

Lyrics by
DR. SEUSS

Music by
ALBERT HAGUE

Welcome Chrisstmas - 2 - 1

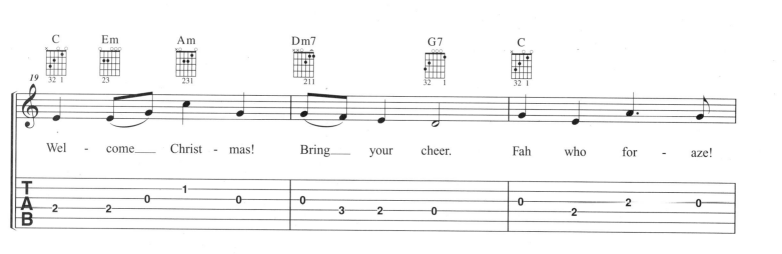

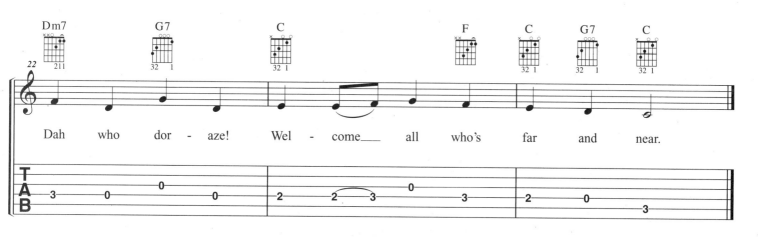

YOU'RE A MEAN ONE, MR. GRINCH

(from *How the Grinch Stole Christmas*)

Lyrics by
DR. SEUSS

Music by
ALBERT HAGUE

Use Suggested Strum Pattern #14

Medium swing

WHEN CHRISTMAS COMES TO TOWN

(from *The Polar Express*)

Words by
GLEN BALLARD

Music by
ALAN SILVESTRI

Use Suggested Strum Pattern #1

Moderately

When Christmas Comes to Town - 3 - 1

TABLATURE EXPLANATION

TAB illustrates the six strings of the guitar.
Notes and chords are indicated by the placement of fret numbers on each string.

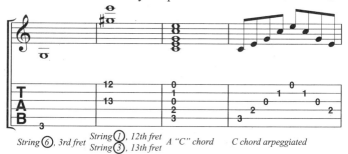

String ⑥, *3rd fret* *String* ①, *12th fret* *A "C" chord* *C chord arpeggiated*
String ③, *13th fret*

BENDING NOTES

Half Step:
Play the note and bend string one half step (one fret).

Whole Step:
Play the note and bend string one whole step (two frets).

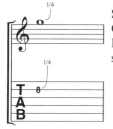

Slight Bend/ Quarter-Tone Bend:
Play the note and bend string sharp.

Prebend and Release:
Play the already-bent string, then immediately drop it down to the fretted note.

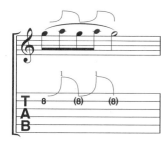

Bend and Release:
Play the note and bend to the next pitch, then release to the original note. Only the first note is attacked.

PICK DIRECTION

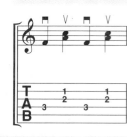

Downstrokes and Upstrokes:
The downstroke is indicated with this symbol (⊓) and the upstroke is indicated with this (V).

ARTICULATIONS

Hammer On:
Play the lower note, then "hammer" your finger to the higher note. Only the first note is plucked.

Pull Off:
Play the higher note with your first finger already in position on the lower note. Pull your finger off the first note with a strong downward motion that plucks the string—sounding the lower note.

Palm Mute:
The notes are muted (muffled) by placing the palm of the pick hand lightly on the strings, just in front of the bridge.

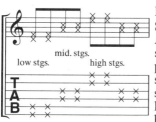

Muted Strings:
A percussive sound is produced by striking the strings while laying the fret hand across them.

Legato Slide:
Play the first note and, keeping pressure applied on the string, slide up to the second note. The diagonal line shows that it is a slide and not a hammer-on or a pull-off.

HARMONICS

Natural Harmonic:
A finger of the fret hand lightly touches the string at the note indicated in the TAB and is plucked by the pick producing a bell-like sound called a harmonic.

RHYTHM SLASHES

Strum Marks/ Rhythm Slashes:
Strum with the indicated rhythm pattern. Strum marks can be located above the staff or within the staff.

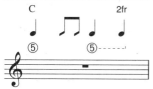

Single Notes with Rhythm Slashes:
Sometimes single notes are incorporated into a strum pattern. The circled number below is the string and the fret number is above.

Artificial Harmonic:
Fret the note at the first TAB number, lightly touch the string at the fret indicated in parens (usually 12 frets higher than the fretted note), then pluck the string with an available finger or your pick.